Choosing To Be
A "What If"
Church

Carol Shanks

Forward

" I have to focus on the day to day responsibilities. The to do list and the hourly calendar are my friends. Face it, there are only 24 hours in my day."

This day-to-day mind set can take a ministry captive. In the captivity of minutia, there is no opportunity to think long term. There is no time for creativity. The focus is on the individual and what that individual can accomplish.

What if we were to focus on what our year-to-year responsibilities are? What if we focused on our responsibilities for this life? What if we went about our life thinking "We all have 24 hours each day. How might we collaborate and make use of all those hours to make a difference in our world?" What if I looked at the to do list and the calendar and asked, "If I didn't do this specific chore/project, would it really matter at the end of the week, the end of the year, the end of my life?

* * * * *

I have told snippets of Bethel's story to a number of people. I love to tell the story because for me this is what the church should be. Each time I told the story, the listener would inevitably tell me "You should write a book about this."

It took a number of years and a number of friends prodding, cajoling, and nagging me to write the Bethel story down. Finally, I had a convicting experience. The experience seared into my heart the need for the Bethel story to be written down.

Grace Church convicted me. I had been asked by their pastor to stop by a meeting at their church one evening to tell the Bethel story. Grace Church was in a gap; a gap between the now and the what is to be. My purpose in telling Bethel's story was to be a Barnabas – an encourager. Every church, but particularly small membership churches, needs encouragement. My hope was that the Bethel story would give Grace the encouragement to continue to slog their way through the gap.

The power of the Bethel story surprised even me that night. I told the story of where Bethel had been, where we were and how we had traversed the bridge to get there.

At the end of the story, there was a Pentecost moment in the room. The people sitting around the table began to speak in tongues. Not tongues of a different language but tongues of a different way of envisioning their church. One person around the table said, "We could do this!" To which I responded, "The purpose in my telling you this story is not for you to do what Bethel did. The purpose in my telling you this story is..." But it was too late. The group was on fire with the Spirit. They were imagining what the next season of their life could look like.

After about five minutes I realized there was no stopping this group. I stood up from the table, picked up a marker, and suggested that I write down some of the things they were saying. I could hardly write fast enough. The group was on fire!

The Grace experience convicted me to write down the Bethel story. If this story can encourage one small church to find new life, I have a responsibility to make sure this story gets told. The telling of this story needed to be a priority on my to do list and calendar.

Thank you to my friend, coach and editor Jill Baker for her suggestions, perseverance, and cheerleading. Thank you to my husband, David, for his tireless proofreading and encouragement. And thank you to the members of Bethel church for their faithful witness as we continue to imagine what's possible when we boldly live out our Christian discipleship.

Carol Shanks
September 2011

Table of Contents

1 - Persistence Pays Off

The phone rang. I was busy wrapping up the last details of an eight-year ministry at a large church. I was ready to go, though bouts of grief washed over me from time to time. I answered the phone and talked with a woman named Elna from a small church about twenty minutes away. The church was looking for a part-time pastor. She had heard I was leaving my current position and wondered if I would be interested in considering the pastoral position at their church. While it warmed my heart, I knew that was not a part of my preferred picture for the future. I gently and kindly thanked her for thinking of me and wished her good luck on their search. "I didn't think you'd be interested. But I thought I'd just ask. What I was wondering is whether you'd be willing to come and meet with our search committee to help us with a mock interview and look over our church profile. It would be good to have a fresh set of eyes to read it."

Now there was something I could say yes to. I love helping people and churches look to their future, look at where their passions and the needs of the world come together. "Sure, I would be happy to do that," I said. Helping with this project also lessened the twinge of guilt I was feeling for saying no to her first offer.

Elna sent me their church profile. Bethel

United Church of Christ. They were a young church, less than 50 years old. In this part of the country they were mere youngsters. The church I was leaving had recently celebrated their 150th anniversary. That kind of longevity was not unusual in this area where German immigrants had settled to farm. But Cahokia was not a German farming settlement. Cahokia has French roots and was one of the first settled areas of the region. Cahokia was a declining, almost urban town in comparison to the German, up and coming community where I had just served. As I drove to Cahokia I realized it was a twenty-minute trip from one culture to another.

The search committee and I met to look at their church profile. We walked through the profile page by page. The committee had done a nice a job of presenting themselves. They were looking for a unique person to serve as their pastor. They were looking for an experienced pastor looking for a part-time position to help them through the process of probably closing the church within a few years.

We decided early in the evening that I would ask them questions and they would ask me questions just as if this were a real interview they were having with a candidate. Afterwards, we could talk about the process and any changes they might want to consider. At the end of the evening after we had debriefed the process, a committee member named Virgil asked, "So, will you consider coming as our pastor?" I remember smiling and saying, "No, this was just a mock interview. I am glad I had the opportunity to come and hopefully be of some help to your committee in this search process." "Yes," Virgil said, "we know this was a mock interview, but set that aside. I'm asking whether you would consider coming and serving as our pastor."

All eyes were on me. I don't remember what kind of backpedaling I did or what kind of "pastorese" I said to them. You know – something about where God is calling me. I do remember thinking as I drove home – who will ever choose to come to that church? Maybe they could find a retired pastor. I thought about how different they were from where I currently served. What nice people – bless their hearts.

A few weeks later Elna called again. Just wanting to see if I had changed my mind. "The committee still talks about you." They had asked her to call and "just make sure". I assured her that my answer was the same, but that I was on the look out for a pastor who might be interested in their little church. I hung up – a bit melancholy. Bless their hearts, again.

The next time Elna called me at home. I had told my husband about this poor little church and how the lady had even called me a second time. My husband answered the phone. "Just a minute." He turned to me, "It's the lady from the church in Cahokia." "You have got to be kidding!" I said. This has to be one of the most persistent people I know.

"Sorry to disturb you at home, but the committee just wanted to double check with you. We really think you are the pastor for us." With a firmer voice I asserted that I was not interested in a part-time pastoral position. "Well, would you be willing to come back and talk to the committee. I think they'd understand better if it was coming from you." You bet. I was willing to stop in at the next committee meeting so I can make my point crystal clear.

The group was in a circle when I arrived. Nice people – just not where I was feeling led to. I explained, "I am finishing work at a church where I was working 60-70 hours a week. I don't know how to work part-time."

"I think I'm being called to youth ministry," knowing they had only two youth in church. I continued, "Even if I were able to put two part-time jobs together, youth ministry is weekend intensive. Sundays are the exact time when you need a pastor." Finally, my rationale was crystal clear. There was a side glance between two members of the committee. Ken asked, "So how many Sundays do you think you'd be gone?"

I thought, "you've got to be kidding!" I started to laugh until I looked at their faces. No one was

—
4

smiling. Bless their hearts. I needed to give them the respect they deserved. But I also needed to make very clear that working in the area of youth ministry I would be away many Sundays. I was not the pastor they were looking for. How could I explain this in a powerful way? I began, "Ok, each year pastors have four weeks of vacation and two weeks of study leave to begin with. That's six Sundays. Working in youth ministry I would be gone probably six other Sundays a year. In other words, twelve Sundays a year. One Sunday a month I would not be here." There. That should do it.

It was quiet. Lips were pursed. They were not looking at me. They were looking at one another. Finally Virgil said, "I think that will work for us."

2- We Really Don't Have A Choice

One thing that truly miffs me is when someone says, "Well, we really don't have a choice." Of course, we have choices. They may not be the choices we like, but we have choices. During those first months at Bethel there seemed to be a common litany. Members: "We really don't have a choice". Pastor: "We always have choices."

The reality was that they felt stuck. They felt that closing the church was the only logical solution. They were so discouraged. Unfulfilled dreams faced us every time we walked in the church door. Literally. Architectural drawings of what the "finished" church would look like still hung in the entryway of the church. The current building was only Phase One back in the early sixties when it was built. The current building was actually going to be a wing of the completed building. Phase Two was to add a larger sanctuary at one end of the current building. And then when Cahokia really boomed with growth, which seemed inevitable in the sixties, there was plenty of ground on the other side of the sanctuary for yet another wing. The architectural drawings were done more than forty years ago. The town had boomed "after the war". (I find it interesting that we talk about "the war" – like our country has only been in one war.)

Cahokia had a housing program where returning veterans could purchase homes with no down payments. Working class families flocked to the area and bought a piece of the American dream. They purchased little houses with two and three bedrooms. They filled them up with children for mother to care for, while father went off to work in St. Louis. No one had a lot of money, but the future looked bright for them and for their children.

That was forty years ago. The future didn't look so bright now. Not at Bethel and not in Cahokia. The search committee had told me "We need a pastor with experience to help us work through the process of closing this church." I had never helped close a church. It was not something I had experience in. Maybe it was the newness that made the endeavor seem like a challenge or even an adventure.

"We need a pastor with experience to help us work through the process of closing this church". I remember that comment from the search committee vividly. But once I arrived on the scene, a case of amnesia seemed to come over the congregation. No one really wanted to talk about the future. Everyone was happy with me as the new pastor. Suddenly no one wanted to talk about closing the church.

I began to wonder whether the comment about closing the church had been just a ploy, a pull on the heartstrings by a desperate search committee. It was the new adventure that had finally drawn me to the church. But now the congregation just wanted to put their heads in the sand regarding the future. They were ready to enjoy the moment.

I visited every family in their home during those first few months. They loved our visits. This was their one on one time with the new pastor. It was time to show off the pictures of their children and grandchildren and maybe even serve me a piece of their favorite recipes. It was also a chance to be candid about their lives and the life of the church without others in earshot.

Bethel folks love to talk. They are willing to talk about pretty much everything to one another. Visitors can be a bit taken aback by the forthrightness of the conversations. Not afraid to share details of personal life, medical conditions, inner thoughts that some folks might think should remain "inner" thoughts and not outer conversation. Joys and concerns time during Morning Prayer at Sunday worship could often be as lengthy and detailed as a sermon.

There were two things that Bethel folks tended not to discuss openly with one another. One of those things was the future. Yet in the sanctuary of their homes they began to open up and talk candidly about the future. Time and time again I heard "If only…" If only we had some young families like years past. If only we had youth. If only we had the finances to keep going. Together we talked about closing the church but often they suggested that we not talk about it openly on Sunday mornings.

Most everyone was certain that they, and maybe one other person, were the only people thinking about how the church would be closing. To talk about it openly seemed like they were disrespecting the charter members who were still among them. It also felt like they were giving up on one another. They loved one another – loved talking with one another, loved worshipping together, and loved eating together. No one wanted to be the one to bring this unhappiness out into the open.

3 - Choices

There are always choices in life. They may not be the ones you like, but there are always choices. There may even be choices you have not yet imagined. That was my message to the congregation during our first year together. It was time to empower this congregation.

There were three things, I believe, that had precipitated talk about closing the church. First, there was the pastoral vacancy. There was a downward swing in the church with no pastoral leadership bringing a word of hope. Second, there was dwindling membership. A church fight some years ago, as well as a changing community, had taken a toll on the congregation. And there was the issue of finances.

Whenever the subject was broached about closing the church, the answer would revolve around money. "Well, we have X amount of money in the savings account. We withdraw X amount to meet the budget each year. So it looks like we have about three years till we close, maybe four if we are very careful with the money."

Our culture has an addiction to numbers. We are always concerned with "How many people were there?" "How large is your congregation?" How large is your budget?" "How much money do you have?" Maybe it was the Depression that brought about this mind set. Maybe it was the prosperity gospel movement. Wherever this addiction comes from, it is not helpful or faithful.

Conversation with the entire congregation was the seedbed for the future. Not everyone enjoyed those conversations. We were talking about painful realities. These conversations were hard work. Strategic dreaming was not a part of life for some members of the congregation who lived life on the edge, just making it from week to week. For many members there was a mindset of "Don't talk about it. What is going to happen, will just happen. Just enjoy the moment." That mindset drove my firmly rooted middle class, privileged mind crazy. Some time later I realized that the "Don't talk, don't plan" mindset is a coping mechanism for people living on the edge. It helps them survive but not flourish. It made absolutely no sense to me. But this was my first visit to the edge.

Upon my arrival to Bethel there was just one choice, close the church. By the time I had visited every household and held a few town hall meetings we had over ten choices. There was still the "close the church and go our separate ways" choice. On the other end of the spectrum there was the choice of moving the congregation to a growing area and building a new church there. Other choices included merging with another congregation, becoming a house church, or creating a multicultural congregation. How would we go about making a choice?

There had been a seismic shift. We had moved from having no choice to having to choose how to proceed. Choices brought about a renewed hope and a sense of responsibility for the future. The tone of Sunday mornings changed from despair to a more edgy "who knows what could happen". There was just a hint of anticipation in the air. We had taken a step away from the edge.

The questions we asked ourselves were the seeds planted in the seedbed of conversations. When the conversation would die down, we would ask a new question. We asked ourselves what we would miss if the church closed. Of course, the fellowship of friends ranked high. Those special holiday worship services made the list, as well as working together at rummage sales. But then we asked the question: what will the wider community miss if we were to close?

Bethel had always been a generous congregation in the community and in the denominational conference. We were known for our emphasis on mission. The community would miss our collaboration with the school and the food pantry, as well as our rummage sales. I believe that asking ourselves the wider community question was the seed that took root and brought us to the choice we made.

Our community needs an agency working to meet the growing needs of struggling families. As Bethel aged, it was very hard for us to continue those community outreach services. Backs and feet ached after rummage sales. We lacked the organizational skills, the finances and the person-power to address the growing number of needs. But maybe a well-established agency could make use of the church building and address some of the needs of our community.

It was at this point that the first "detail" crept into our conversation. How could an agency afford to purchase this building? Some members served as volunteers with helping agencies. Some members served on boards of directors of service agencies. The service agencies were always in fundraising mode. What made us think that an agency had the money to purchase this building? Then one of the wise elders asked, "Well, what are we going to do with the money? We're closing." Someone else piped up "Maybe we could hang on a little longer with that money." Someone else laughingly said "Or maybe we just give the agency the building. If they're willing to do the hard work that's needed here, just give them the building." So giving the building away to an agency became another option on our list of choices.

On the heels of the first detail came the next detail. I don't recall if it was the church historian or an attorney in the congregation who sent us searching through the by-laws. There we found our by-laws indicated if the congregation were to cease to be a church, the building was to be given to the Illinois South Conference. We had a healthy relationship with the conference. We were happy to give the building to the conference. But if the final choice were to give or sell the building to someone other than the conference, we would need to address the by-law issue.

We could have been plunged prematurely into legalities. But we chose not to let that legal issue minimize our list of choices at this point. It was, after all, just a brainstorming list. Once you start addressing details, the creative juices stop flowing. Once you begin the "We can't because…" then the possibilities of " what if…" begin to dry up.

We used the tools of congregational conversations and straw polls as we began to cull down the list of choices. It worked well to begin identifying our least favorite choices. This process brought about consensus on which choices to set aside for the moment.

The option of selling or giving the building away continued to be on the short list of possibilities.

It was time to bring the rest of the family into the details of our conversations. I had been in surface conversations with our Conference Minister, conversations about my walk with this new congregation. Like most conference ministers, he was happy to have one less congregation on the list of those searching for pastoral leadership. It was an added bonus when congregation and pastor seemed to be working together in collegial ways.

When I shared our process with the Conference Minister, he was excited and supportive. I recall a conversation about the conference not being a real estate agency. The conference had no reason to want an empty church building, especially in a depressed area. So with the conference's prayerful blessing, we continued on in this process of preparing our funeral.

Through consensus we had narrowed the list down to choices we were willing to live or die with. Finally a vote was taken. It was a paper ballot vote. The thought of a show of hands was just too divisive and emotional for the congregation.

Debbie and Graham quietly counted the votes

at a table in front of the congregation. It was a clear, though not unanimous, vote. The congregation voted to **give** the building to a mission agency. There was a huge sigh of relief and an ominous sense that something of great meaning had just transpired. This gifting would be the first step in preparing ourselves to end the ministry, to close, to die – or so we thought.

4 - Agency Dating

There was a huge sense of relief. A choice had been made and voted on. We had worked so long and hard to get to this point. But the work was far from over. It's hard work to die... especially to CHOOSE to die. The next step was to come up with a list of agencies that we might give the building to.

We began by looking at the needs of our community. We prayed. We prayed to have a clear vision of the needs of our community. We prayed that the right agency would emerge through the process.

It was great to be at this point in the process. We had identified three agencies we believed had the mission needed to serve our community. There was consensus within the congregation that any of these three agencies would do a great job. It was time to begin the "dating" process and see who would grasp the vision, have the passion to serve our community, and receive our gift.

As the pastor, I found myself being a bit protective of my flock. They had worked so tirelessly to get to this point in their dying process. They had been so brave. They were in many ways, proud of themselves.

I didn't want one of these dates to crush their dreams. What if they dated all three and none of the agencies wanted the building or none of them wanted to expand their services in our area? I think the congregation felt that anxiety as well. I was relieved when a few of the consistory members suggested I check out these agencies to see if they had any initial interest.

One of the agencies worked with women and their families who were survivors of domestic violence. Domestic violence was an issue that plagued our area. It was an issue that had touched lives in our congregation. People felt very positive about this agency partner. I called the Executive Director of the agency, who I had met in the past. I explained that I needed to sit down and share an exciting project with her.

We met in a coffee shop over breakfast. I was nervous. This certainly felt like a date. Sure, she knew me. But would she and her agency want to get in a serious relationship with Bethel?

We began our breakfast catching me up on all the wonderful growth that was happening with their agency. The need for their ministry was expanding. A new house was being rehabbed for the women and their children.

As she spoke with passion about the families they served, my heart was soaring. Here is a person who is passionate about the mission of her agency. She was working tirelessly. She was thinking outside the box. She was taking the next steps to expand the services of their agency. This was it! It felt right. Now it was my turn to talk about Bethel.

Like a swooning parent, I talked about this amazing congregation. I outlined their passion to serve the community. I shared how brave they had been in considering their future. And then I shared about their extravagant generosity – wanting to give their property and building to an agency. I talked about our process. And then I shared that her agency had been chosen as one of our three finalists. The director was amazed!

She said she was honored for her agency to have been chosen. We talked about Cahokia. We talked about how we were a great match. At first, it was magic. But as we continued to talk a major roadblock seemed to emerge.

Their agency worked in the state of Missouri. Our church building was in the state of Illinois. It's not that it couldn't be done. But working across state lines on legislation and working with state agencies from two states would be a level of expansion which their agency was not in a position to take on. If they were given a building in Illinois, their Board of Directors would want to sell the building to fund their current sites in Missouri. And we both knew that was not what we wanted. As the breakfast came to an end, we knew we were just going to be friends.

I went back to my car to leave. All of a sudden

I was exhausted. The two-hour breakfast had been emotionally draining. I remembered our prayer that clarity come to us regarding which agency to choose. Our prayer was being answered. I was glad that I had told the consistory I would report out after I had made the initial three visits. I didn't want them to be disappointed that their gift had been rebuffed.

5 - Hoyleton Imagines
What's Possible

Sometimes we present our idea to people or agencies and it feels like we are an entrepreneur seeking a business partner or a funding source. Other times we present our idea to someone and it feels like talking to family. Hoyleton Youth and Family Services was family. Having grown up in the Illinois South Conference of our denomination, I had supported Hoyleton since I was a young child by collecting offerings for Christmas gifts and back-to-school items. I had experienced plenty of picnics and auctions, banquets and walk-a-thons with Hoyleton.

When I shared with the Executive Director that Bethel was looking for a mission agency to give their building to, it was like preparing popcorn. There was the initial first pop or two... yes, they were interested. As the conversation continued, idea after idea popped forth regarding ways which Hoyleton could make use of Bethel's extravagant gift. They imagined offices with counseling sessions; foster care meetings, and staff trainings. We toured the community noting numerous social service needs. The popcorn bag (or pan – depending on your age) was about to overflow with newly burst kernels of popcorn. Hoyleton was imagining all sorts of possibilities for the church building and meeting the needs of the community.

Giving the building to Hoyleton was like leaving the building to your grandchildren. It was still going to be in the family. Hoyleton had the same DNA as Bethel, to put the "least of these among us" as the top priority.

Hoyleton has always imagined what was possible for the youth and families they served, no matter how severe their circumstances seemed. Imagining possibilities was in their DNA. Hoyleton began to imagine not just having a new building and new ministries at that site. They began to imagine a partnership with Bethel.

Mission giving was part of Bethel's DNA. Mission giving is what had brought them to this point in their story. Were there regrets in their life? Certainly. There always are. How they wished the community had developed in different directions. But now in these last years of their life, they were at peace, content to turn their building over to Hoyleton for continued use.

It was invigorating to hear Hoyleton's passion and enthusiasm for ministry. This was exactly what we had hoped and prayed for. But then Hoyleton imagined something even greater. Something Bethel had never considered. Hoyleton's director encouraged Bethel to continue to make use of the building for worship, until such time as we wished to officially end our ministry. He also asked Bethel to be an active partner with Hoyleton in their new ministry endeavors.

The first official vote of the congregation in this process had been the vote to explore giving our building to a mission agency. At the point of the first vote, everything seemed hypothetical. The second vote was different. We had dated the agencies. When our dating with Hoyleton was getting serious, the Executive Director had come to Bethel to worship with us and to answer questions. The second vote, like the first, was a paper ballot, voting to give the building and surrounding property to Hoyleton Ministries to make use of as they saw fit. The only string attached was that the building and property would be given to the Illinois South Conference in the event that Hoyleton ceased to exist.

I had always envisioned the day of the vote being a sad day. But instead of feeling like a day when the breathing machines were turned off, it felt like the resuscitation paddles had been applied to Bethel. This was the official day of voting. There was a quiet anticipation in the air. The ballots were handed out. As Georgia played the organ, we prayed and voted. The ballots were collected in offering plates and placed on a table in front of the congregation.

The votes were counted aloud by the consistory chairperson. Debbie's hand and voice shook as she unfolded and read the first ballot. "Yes". The ballot was handed to Graham. Graham, a charter member, had been on the building committee when the church was built. Graham looked at each ballot and then made a mark on a tally sheet. Debbie's voice grew stronger as she read time after time "Yes. Yes. Yes." The vote to give our building to Hoyleton was unanimous. Much hard work had gone into reaching that point. And much hard work was still ahead of us.

And what happened to the third agency we had considered giving the building to? Puentes de Esperanza decided Cahokia was too far away from the emerging center of Hispanic population. But interestingly, just a year or so later, they became an official ministry of Hoyleton.

6 - Details

The initial season of this visioning process was filled with excitement and adrenalin. There were options and possibilities and imagining. This was the energizing part. Now came the season of fact and figures, environmental consultations, attorneys, and original building blueprints (where are those anyway?). We were a congregation of faithful, visionary people without many legal or business skills. But we found others who were willing to help us through this important season.

It was a time of great learning for me as the still relatively new pastor of this congregation. To transfer real estate, we had to make sure there were no liens on the property. That shouldn't a problem. A quick inquiry at the county courthouse will check that item off our list. False.

We found the denomination had given our congregation money as a new church start more than 40 years ago. The granting agency of the denomination still had a lien on the building.

There were hours… days of searching through church records. First and foremost it reminded me how important it is to retain and accurately file church papers. The best I can say on our behalf is "There were files". As for others' files, the new church grant occurred during the time of the merger that formed the United Church of Christ (UCC). I cannot imagine all the shifting of files that had to occur in creating the new offices of this new denomination. It was a lesson in history regarding how a new church start began in the late 1950's.

One of things that I was most thankful for was the founding pastor, Rev. Herb Schafale and the charter members of Bethel who were still around and able to help in sorting through events that occurred during the early years. These were not issues of neglect or any sense of impropriety. Who would be thinking about issues of giving a church away when they were in the act of starting a church in a booming community?

The denominational lien was one of the details where Bethel congregation showed her true colors. After many phone calls and emails with the UCC offices in Cleveland and our Illinois South Conference office, it was determined that these grants/loans were no longer subject to repayment. Both the national church and the Conference were overjoyed that an agency of the UCC Council for Health and Human Service Ministries would be given our building. What great news! When I shared the news with the congregation, they had other thoughts.

Remember, we had charter members who were still active in the congregation. They told stories

of how Pastor Schafale had walked through the
community knocking on doors and inviting
people to come worship at this new church.
Bethel rented a small building the first two
years. As the congregation grew, so did their
need for a church building. They remembered
how the national church had supported them in
those early years, how the national church had
believed in them and their new community.
They remembered making payments to the
national church early on. Then there was
fuzziness as to when or why our payments
stopped.

Bethel members appreciated that the national
church was willing to forego payment of this last
portion of the new church grant. But there were
other issues to consider. We did not want
Hoyleton to think that we had skirted some
moral obligation to repay the church grant. We
also thought about all the new church starts that
need to begin now. After very little
conversation, the congregation voted to make
good on this bill. They happily voted to pay that
last several thousand dollars. I was so proud to
be a part of this congregation. These are people
firmly grounded within the United Church of
Christ. Always were and always would be.
That is good news in an area where
congregations sometime second guess and
question the faithfulness of our denomination.

There were plenty of legal i's to dot and t's to

cross. An attorney representing Hoyleton drew up all the necessary legal papers. Bethel members had a friend who was an attorney who was willing to review the agreements pro bono. There was the environmental assessment of the building and the property. And then came an emotionally hard part.

Even though Bethel's congregation was going to continue to worship in the building, the building was not ours. I felt a responsibility to Hoyleton and to the congregation to make certain the congregation understand the ramifications of this decision. We had talked about it time and time again prior to the vote. Now the vote had occurred and it was time to live out this agreement. It was time to get rid of all the "stuff" that had accumulated in the church building over these forty some years.

"The building is no longer Bethel's. We must clean out the church building and prepare to hand it over to Hoyleton. We would be allowed to have an office in the rear of the building where altar paraments, files and flower arrangements could be stored. We would have a set of cabinets in the kitchen to store our fellowship supplies. But the building was now Hoyleton's. They could make use of it as they saw fit.

Throughout the building, there were shelves and cabinets full of "stuff" that needed to be gotten rid of. Some of the items had not been used for years. Broken crayons, used curriculum, pieces of games, the angel's headband – every church has stuff like this. Some of the items were used occasionally. Some of the items had deeply sentimental value. We returned hand made items to the families of those who had made them. After returning hand-made items, there was a Sunday when remaining items were on display and each of us could take an item or two

This was an emotional process for us. Getting rid of these items helped us as a congregation realize that we were dying. Until we began that cleaning out process, we could not face the sort of transition to death that this act of surrender meant for us. And until we died, we were not ready for resurrection.

7 - A Wedding at a Funeral

Was it a funeral or was it a wedding? The process had begun with the congregation planning our funeral; planning the end of our ministry. I had been called to serve as pastor with Bethel church in September 2001. We began the hard work of being intentional about the future of our ministry. In March 2003 Bethel formally gave their church building to Hoyleton. It had been eighteen months of tireless work and faithful conversations.

Because Bethel Church and Hoyleton Ministries were both active members of the Illinois South Conference of the United Church of Christ, we chose to share this new partnership with our broader church family. On a Sunday afternoon we hosted a partnership celebration. The cast of participants for the event were carefully chosen. Each played a special and symbolic role.

The Reverend Herb Schafale is the founding pastor of Bethel. He had just graduated from Eden Theological Seminary when he felt led to begin a new church. He and his wife Bennie had given years of their lives to Bethel. Currently, Herb served the Minister of Visitation at an area congregation.

Even though Herb had been supportive of my leadership throughout this process, I had always found it difficult to talk with him. I always felt a bit guilty, a bit of sadness, when I thought about the impending death of this, his first congregation. Herb led us in prayer that afternoon.

The Reverend Krista Betz is a daughter of the Bethel congregation. She currently served as pastor of a United Church of Christ congregation in Augusta, Missouri. Her grandparents, Erwin and Matilda Betz were charter members. Krista had grown up surrounded by Bethel's love and nurture. This shining star of the congregation opened the service with the call to worship.

Guy Baney is a current member of Bethel, an every Sunday member who faithfully serves as our treasurer and lector. This decision would affect his life each and every week. Guy read the scripture lesson at the partnership celebration.

The Reverend Jerry Paul, the President and CEO of The Deaconess Foundation, shared the message at the celebration. Jerry is viewed as a visionary leader who walked with Deaconess Health Systems through transformational seasons and birthed the Deaconess Foundation. He was also one of the interim pastors early in Bethel's life.

I shared with our gathered family and friends the story of Bethel's recent journey. Then I called upon Graham Rosenberger to present the building blueprints to Hoyleton. Graham had been the chairman of the Building Committee when the church was built. I was elated that Graham could be the person to hand over those architectural drawings that he had spent so much time helping to create. Graham was literally a foundational charter member, active in every part of Bethel's current ministry, especially mission outreach. Just six months later, Graham would die. But he had been so excited to be a part of this season of Bethel's ministry.

Debbie Cupples, the President of the Bethel Consistory, handed Hoyleton the keys to the building. Debbie remembers pulling back her hand full of keys. Cleo Terry, a Hoyleton representative, had said to her "We'll take good care of her," to which Debbie said "I know you will" and tearfully handed her the keys.

Mayor Dee Reed represented the Cahokia community at the celebration. She shared words commending the Bethel congregation for her years of community service and welcoming Hoyleton to the community.

Interim Conference Minister of the Illinois South Conference, the Reverend Christine Boardman, was present to give the conference's blessing as well as to accept the afternoon's offering that would go toward new church starts.

The afternoon ended with wonderful fellowship, refreshments and reminising.

For me as Bethel's pastor, this was the time when the ministry shift became reality. Maybe it had been the rituals of the afternoon or maybe it was real because now everyone knew. For whatever reason, finally deep within my heart I knew there was no turning back. But I was still uncertain whether I was feeling the grief of a funeral or the tender sadness of a wedding.

8 - Selling the Farm

Bethel is a mix of urban and rural. The church building is in a village that most would consider urban. We also have a rural connection through the farmland we own. We became farmers through a serendipitous turn of events. The farmland had been a gift from someone we did not know. One of our former members was a real estate broker. She met a farmer in need of a tax break. He wanted to get rid of some farmland. Ruth suggested the farmer give the piece of land to a non-profit agency. He didn't have any such agency in mind so Ruth suggested her church. In a nutshell, that is how we came to own farmland.

Each year an area farmer plants most of the twenty acres. The church then receives a nice check from the farmer for a portion of the yield. Each year the check is divided between several agencies that feed people. As their new pastor, I wondered out loud why the church doesn't consider keeping a portion of the proceeds for the expenses of the church.

Their answer to my question is a snapshot into the way Bethel people think. "Why don't we keep a portion of the farm income? It just doesn't seem right. We didn't purchase the land. The land was given to us. The land was a gift. It seems like we should pass on the gift to others. Since the land is planted in crops, hunger projects seem to make the most sense."

Their answer to my question is also a snapshot into the way Bethel people choose to live out their faith, trusting God to be faithful as we do our part to be faithful servants.

Now, a bit about this land. The land is in a strange configuration. The parcels are divided by a two lane paved street and a six lane interstate highway. Much of the land is in a flood plain. The whole town of Cahokia is in a flood plain, but our land more so than other sections.

In the midst of preparing to close the church we realized that we would need to dispose of this farmland. While Ruth had died several years ago, there was a member who had a sister who was a real estate broker who was willing to help us sell the farmland.

True to Bethel's spirit, selling the land was not our first choice. There had been a plan to give a portion of the land to Habitat for Humanity. Seemed like the perfect plan. Several Bethel members had worked on Habitat projects. The Habitat chapter in the neighboring town didn't want land in another town. Bethel didn't want to begin a Habitat chapter in Cahokia when the church was coming to an end. Without getting too political, and Cahokia is a very political town, several village leaders told us that Cahokia didn't need any Habitat houses.

About that time a housing developer came forward interested in the land. After all the surveys, the developer decided he actually would purchase only a portion of the land. We were disappointed. We needed to be rid of all the land. But the decision was to settle for the offer.

With the sale pending, Bethel was about to experience what potentially could have led to a big problem, or so I thought. I talked with the congregation. "This sale is going to bring Bethel $32,000. That is a big chunk of money. More money than the church has ever had at one time. Money can be divisive. Money can cause problems and hurt feelings. So we need to be very intentional and talk openly about how to make use of this money," I told them.

A congregation conversation was held to discuss how to best use the proceeds of the farmland sale. The congregation was always relaxed about "just talking" with one another. We knew there were no votes at these gatherings, just opportunities for everyone to share their opinions and ideas.

The first idea on how to use the money sounded like a good one – we all take a vacation! After some bubbly conversation we realized we were not going to be able to decide *where* to vacation. The laughter was a good starting place. It reminded us of what a blessed situation we were in.

Someone wondered aloud what would have happened if this land deal had happened earlier. We would have had money. Would we have thought about giving our building away and closing the church? You could see this question had people thinking. Then the conversation began to bubble over once again. "This is the happiest we have been in a long time." "We wouldn't be in this great partnership with Hoyleton". Even if we had money, we would still have old guys up on the roof, who didn't need to be up on the roof." "Think of the mission opportunities this is going to give us. We can use this money the way we want to and not give it to the power company." "God knew what he was doing with this timing."

Now that we had that elephant out of the room, we could begin to think about how to utilize this amazing gift. The congregation met in four small groups, each led by a consistory member. There were three questions that were discussed. What percentage of the money from the sale of the farmland should we keep? What ideas do you have for the money we will give away? What ideas do you have for the money we will keep for Bethel?

After talking and listening there seemed to be a

consensus. Seventeen people participated in the conversation. Twelve thought that we should keep 50% of the money. One person thought we should give all the proceeds away. On the other end of the spectrum, one person thought we should invest the money and use the interest for benevolences. Two people thought we should keep 25% and one person thought we should keep 70% of the proceeds.

The conversation was thoughtful. Everyone voiced their opinions and respected the opinions of others. It did not take long before consensus was reached.

The next issue discussed was not so easy; which agencies and project should receive grants. We felt like family with many of the nine agencies we suggested. We had a discussion on how much to give to each group. A month later there was a congregational meeting to vote on dispersing 50% ($16,000) of the revenue from the sale of a section of the farmland. The vote was unanimous. At that same congregational meeting there was a vote on the agencies and the amount to be given to each. Since much conversation had occurred around the fellowship table and at prior meetings, it was not too surprising the vote to fund the following projects was unanimous.

- Pastoral Library Grants to Eden Theological Seminary students
- Urban Gardening Grants to Metro Hope in East St. Louis
- Adapt a Classroom in a Cahokia School
- Habitat for Humanity House in memory of Rev. Buck Jones
- Youth Mission Trip Grants to UCC youth groups
- Disaster Relief Grant for One Great Hour of Sharing
- Domestic Violence Grant to Southwestern Illinois Violence Prevention Center
- An International Focused Grant –adopting a child outside the United States

Over a three-year period, we enjoyed working on these programs. For some organizations, it meant a one-time check. For others, it involved much more. Several of us served as reading tutors on a weekly basis for the classroom we adopted at Elizabeth Morris grade school for three years. Several of us worked on the Habitat for Humanity house that honored a dear friend and justice advocate, the Rev. Buck Jones.

Because many Eden Seminary students doing field education, as well as Eden graduates had served Bethel, we wanted to express our thanks. We offered a grant for students to begin their pastoral libraries. To help us with our decision as to who should receive the grant, we asked interested students to write us a brief essay sharing the importance and the joy of ministry in a small membership church. We read fourteen statements over a two-year period and presented four awards. Recipients visited Bethel so we had the opportunity to meet them and hear about their dream for ministry in the church.

The tip of the iceberg for us as a congregation was the Youth Mission Trip Grant. Little did we know what a mustard seed of a grant this would be.

9 - Youth Ministry With No Youth

The idea of giving mission grants from proceeds of the land sale started when we thought about who we are and how we wanted to make use of this huge, for us, one time influx of money. Giving away half of the proceeds to serve those in need was true to who we were and who we wanted to continue to be. We had always been knee-deep in mission work. We thought of all the wonderful mission projects we had been a part of. I shared with Bethel how church youth groups often raise money so they can go on mission trips and help others. . That is exactly the kind of thing Bethel wanted to do, if only we had youth in our congregation.

"If only…" those are two very dangerous words in the church. "If only… if only we had more members. " "If only we were in a growing area." " If only we had talented leadership." "If only…" cast a depressed pall over us. In contrast, the words "What if…." have a whole different effect. "What if" sparks imagination. "What if" guides you outside the lines, the lines that may stifle your creativity.

Early on in my ministry with Bethel, members of the congregation went to a concert at another church. We heard an amazing musician and man of faith, Ken Medema. Here was a man who refused to look at limitations. Instead he looked at only possibilities. Ken is a gifted pianist and songwriter who happens to be blind. One of Ken's songs is "Color Outside the Lines". We were reminded of that song as we talked about thinking outside the box regarding our mission grants. We needed to stop thinking about what we didn't have and instead focus on possibilities – coloring outside the lines.

What if we kept our mission spirit alive by making grants to other churches' youth groups who were raising money to go on mission trips? What if we then invited them to come to Bethel and report on their mission trip? What if youth ministry became a focus for Bethel... even though we had no youth? And so our youth ministry program began. Little did we realize how much our youth ministry would expand our horizons.

Where would we find these youth groups? We looked first to our family – our Illinois South Conference family. It takes a village to raise a child. It takes a Conference to raise children with the seeds of mission partnerships planted deep within them. We sent invitations to churches asking their youth groups to apply for a Bethel grant to help fund their mission trip. We wanted to know where they were going on their mission trip, what they planned to do, what other fundraising they had done, and why this trip was important to them.

Bethel sponsored several youth mission trips

over the three years of the grants. It was more than just a check in the mail. Once the youth group was selected, we began a prayer circle for the group. We sent them a card right before they left for their trip. And then we anxiously awaited their visit to tell us about how their mission experience had affected their lives. We watched videos and scoured photo albums drinking in the excitement of these youth in our family. Finally the grant dollars were all spent. It was good while it lasted. If only we could keep up the youth mission trip ministry. (Those two words – "if only…" they creep back into our vocabulary in the church so easily.)

Youth ministry was one of my passions. Youth ministry was in fact, my other part-time ministry job. While I was pastor at Bethel, I also was serving as the part-time Youth and Young Adult Minister of the Missouri Mid-South Conference of the United Church of Christ, just over the river in St. Louis. That ministry kept me connected with youth leaders throughout the conference.

As I listened to youth ministers talk about their mission trip experiences, too often I heard stories of "if only…." If only we could have great service opportunities with progressive Christian theology. If only we could meet more people on our trips. If only agencies were more organized and prepared for mission trip groups. If only we could sustain the mission trip high once we got back home. I heard this same litany of "if onlys" from three different leaders within a couple week period. These were seasoned leaders with a real passion for youth ministry. If they were struggling with these issues, so were a majority of youth ministers. I began to pray for insight on how to help these leaders and their youth groups.

One afternoon I visited with my friend Joan who directs a food pantry. Early in her life, she had also been a youth minister. Our ministry paths were such that we could finish one another's sentences. We didn't have a chance to talk often, but when we did talk a creative energy emerged. We stood talking shop in the basement of a struggling urban congregation that housed Joint Neighborhood Ministry.

I shared an emerging dream; What if mission trip groups met and worked with only the best service agencies? What if mission trip groups met youth from churches in the city they were visiting? What if mission trip groups would cook their own food since it helps form community? And, their leaders know best what sort of things they will and won't eat. What if the host church would provide recreation for the visiting youth one evening so youth group leaders could have a couple hours of down time/alone time? What if groups would lead their own devotional times each day resourced with materials provided to leaders before their arrival? What if mission trip groups would pay to stay in urban churches and bolster the struggling budgets of those churches?

As I was waxing eloquently, painting the "what if" picture, Pastor Mary happened to appear. Pastor Mary had the heart of a gifted, compassionate urban pastor, but had little youth ministry experience. Joan quickly summarized my dream and then like a lightening bolt had hit her said, "Carol, have you seen the third floor of this building?" I had been in the building numerous times – in the basement, in the sanctuary, but never on the third floor. "Mary, we have got to show her the third floor". As we trekked our way up the stairs, Pastor Mary talked about how they hoped to find a non-profit agency that would rent a portion of the third floor to help them with their financial woes. The only thing urban churches have plenty of is ministry opportunities. The one thing most urban churches are short on are finances.

Upstairs we walked into a space with two smaller rooms, which opened to a large meeting room. Joan and I looked at one another and said, "This is perfect!" Pastor Mary looked a bit bewildered as Joan and I talked in fast, clipped sentences as we brought the space alive to the possibility of a mission trip ministry. One small room to sleep guys and one small room to sleep girls. They open to a large area for gathering and discussion. Down stairs is the kitchen. Our ideas were multiplying.

It sounded like a perfect match. But remember we are church leaders accustomed to creating the never ending "if only" scenarios. If only we had showers at the church. Well, there is a YMCA nearby. Maybe we could use their showers. What if we asked them to partner with us in this project?

Pastor Mary liked the idea. She appreciated the energy of these two youth ministry veterans. But then she reminded us "This all sounds great. But we need to be able to bring in some revenue." Joan and I began to laugh. You see Pastor Mary didn't know how much some of the professional mission trip coordinating agencies charge. When we told her, Mary was in shock. "You mean these youth groups would pay for this service?" Within a month, Pastor Mary had taken the seed of an idea to her church council and Urban Mission Experience-St. Louis (UME-STL) began to blossom forth.

And yes, the YMCA did partner with us. They offered free use of their showers for the visiting youth groups. If the church building had a shower, it would have taken hours for a youth group to all get showered. The church would have been paying the water and gas bill. Instead, within a half hour the entire youth group was showered. What a great partnership!

So why is the story of UME-STL in the midst of Bethel's story? After four years, UME-STL needed an additional church partner for the program. There were weeks in the summer where UME-STL was turning groups away because of lack of space at Epiphany UCC where Pastor Mary served. The UME-STL board began searching for just the right church to absorb the overflow of this successful summer program. They were looking for an urban church in a relatively safe area that loved youth and embraced a progressive Christian theology. They wanted a partner who was willing and able to provide only the most organized and welcoming experience. They were looking for a congregation with a heart for mission.

I shared this mission opportunity with Bethel. We once again began to paint the "What if" picture. We were chosen by UME-STL to be a satellite site for those times when Epiphany was full.   In 2010 we hosted our first UME-STL group – a group that captured our hearts.

10 - A Powerful Pentecost

People often ask us how we became an Open and Affirming congregation. Becoming Open and Affirming was just another day in the life of Bethel church.

It was not a controversial, church-splitting decision. There were no fights; few tense words and no one left the church over it. That in and of itself made it a very big deal in the Midwest. The story goes like this.

Once upon a time, on a bright sunny Pentecost Sunday, the wind of the Holy Spirit came blowing through Bethel Church. The wind had started the day before at my desk. I was trying to write a sermon for Pentecost that just wasn't coming together. I stopped and read over the scripture passage again – slowly, deliberately. I read over that Pentecost passage in Acts several times prayerfully. Of course, I knew the passage. I had been a pastor for some twenty-five Pentecost's.

I went back to the computer and began to type. Only this time the words came quickly. I wasn't thinking about what to write. The words were just flowing through my fingers onto the keyboard. As this continued, I became anxious. I had never had this sort of sermon writing experience before. Growing in anxiety, I took a break, went for a ride and then came back to finish the sermon.

On that Pentecost Sunday, I was anxious about the message that had been given to me. As I walked to the front of the sanctuary I greeted a member of our consistory. I remember saying to Dennis " Please pray for me and this morning's sermon and hang onto your seat." He looked at me, nodded yes and smiled. I had his attention.

During that Pentecost sermon I asked who might the outsiders be today. It was one of those preacher questions – the ones that we ask but don't intend for anyone to answer – at least not out loud. I talked about gay and lesbian people who are often excluded from the church. The United Church of Christ encourages us to study how our church can be open to all people, but especially gay and lesbian people. I pondered aloud if maybe this was the time for our congregation to talk about and study this issue.

Following the sermon and a hymn, we have the sharing of our joys and concerns as we then lift them up in prayer. People laugh that sometimes the joys and concerns can be as long as the sermon. This is the time when we become most vulnerable to one another. We have grown so close that we often share deeply and with great detail.

On this Sunday a number of hands shot up in the air to be called on for the sharing of their joys. Elna spoke up 'I'm glad that we are going to study becoming an Open and Affirming congregation." I think I stopped breathing for a moment. I am certain there was a hint of a smile on my face. But I didn't want to overreact because I was certain there would be people sitting in the congregation who probably did not consider this upcoming study to be a joy.

The floodgates had been opened. Next JoAnn shared her joy of having a church where her niece who is a lesbian could come to worship. It has always been so tough for her niece. She just couldn't understand how people, especially church people could be so mean spirited. Didn't Jesus say, "Love one another"?

Shirley raised her hand to say that her neighbors were gay. They were the best neighbors they have ever had. Dianna talked of caring about family friends who were gay.

It was hard for me to hold back the floodgate of joyful tears welling up inside me. What a remarkable congregation! In a congregation where I had served previously, there had been a special meeting to talk with me after I had preached a sermon from Galatians 3: 28 saying that there was neither Jew or Greek, slave or free, male or female, gay or straight in Christ. So this sermon had been a real step of faith for me. Of course, my Bethel family did not know that part of my history. Nor did the congregation really know these pieces of history that many of their Bethel friends were carrying.

The next Tuesday was Ladies Lunch Out. Once a month the women of Bethel, the ones who were retired, went out to lunch together. When I arrived Pat was the only one at the restaurant. After a few pleasantries Pat said "About this gay thing…" I quietly took a deep breath and thought "OK, here it comes. Not everyone is going to be onboard initially. That's to be expected. So now comes the education." Then Pat said, "About this gay thing, why has our church taken so long to talk about this? " My relief had me laughing out loud.

"No, I'm serious. Why have we not dealt with this issue before now? This is not something new for the UCC. But I can never remember us addressing this." After a thoughtful pause I had to admit, "It's because your pastor is a chicken. I have some scars from another congregation who was adamantly against it." "Against talking about it?" "Oh, my dear Pat. Where do I even begin? Yes, against even talking about it."

Over the next four months we spent time studying scripture, listening to speakers regarding homosexuality, as well as listening and talking with one another. Initially, there were members who felt that a study should not be a necessary part of declaring ourselves Open and Affirming. "You mean we have to study to decide whether to be open and affirming of all

God's children? That makes no sense! This is just who we are already."

Together we discussed the importance of understanding the ramifications of this decision for our congregation, our conference and our community. We wondered out loud whether there might be backlash from our community. We had read about hate crimes against congregations who had taken bold inclusive stances. Each conversation took us back to our faith. What would Jesus want us to do?

Numerous open conversations uncovered that not every member of the church was totally in favor of becoming open and affirming. We listened carefully and compassionately to one another. One member shared that this might be the last straw for him. He was definitely the most conservative member of the congregation. But he was also our friend and valued member of the congregation. My calm response to his last straw comment was "We would really hate to see you leave." And the conversation continued. It was important that everyone be heard. It was also important not to allow a single opinion to take the congregation hostage.

On the day of the congregational vote, I took several of the strong supporters of the ONA stance aside. This would be a historic day for the congregation, no matter which way the vote went. We needed to be mindful of everyone's feelings. Unless the vote was a unanimous yes, we really shouldn't be breaking out in song after the vote. They agreed.

At the end of the worship service, ballots were distributed. Two members of the consistory and myself went to the church office to count the votes. When we returned, fellowship and refreshments were under way. I went to the microphone and shared the results. There had been one no vote and one abstaining vote. We were officially an Open and Affirming congregation. Refreshment time continued. And for the record, no one left the church because of the vote.

11 - A Musical Miracle

Worship is central to Bethel Church. It is when we gather to be fed at Christ's table, fed through God's Word and fed by the love and care of one another. We depend on our organist to help set the tone for worship. We were blessed to have Georgia as our organist when I arrived. But within a few years, Georgia found the need to move to a nursing home outside of Cahokia.

Her move created what seemed like a disaster in the making. Finding a church musician is often a struggle for small congregations. Maybe this was the domino that would cause everything to tumble. Maybe this would be the end of Bethel.

We had enjoyed a sense of revival after entering our partnership with Hoyleton. But the loss of our organist was a deep blow. There were no members who could play the organ. We were not strong singers and had depended on the organ accompaniment to guide us. Dave and Bill would often sing a duet, accompanied by Dave and his guitar. The congregation appreciated their gift of song. But there was still the sense that maybe the loss of our organist was the beginning of the end for this worshipping community.

I had put the word out in church circles hoping for a lead. I had also sent a help wanted ad to a community college. After a few weeks of not even a nibble, I received a phone call from an interested college student. I was pleased but could not have begun to imagine what was about to unfold for us. Over the phone I began asking David questions. I asked if he played the organ (not many people do). Yes, he played the organ and in fact, was an organ major in college. "Tell me about your organ playing experience." He had been playing since grade school. Both his mother and his grandmother played the organ for churches.

I held my breath as I asked if he was willing to accept only a small salary. He was excited to have the opportunity to play the organ. I explained that we were a small United Church of Christ congregation. His voice shared his excitement as he explained he was a member of a UCC church and had grown up in small churches. I was in shock. This was just too good to be true! Here is a young, talented organist excited about serving a small congregation within his own denomination.

Before we could hang up from that first phone conversation, I had to let him know what this congregation was in the midst of deciding. I shared that Bethel was a progressive UCC congregation and that within the next few weeks we were planning to vote to become an Open and Affirming Congregation. I explained exactly what that meant. I talked about the congregation's willingness and excitement over welcoming gay, lesbian, and transgender individuals and their families into our congregation. As pastor, I had to have my only staff member comfortable with this decision. I realized that in conservative southern Illinois this might be the end of our conversation. I paused. There was silence on the other end of the phone. Finally David spoke up " This is amazing. This is exactly the kind of church my girlfriend and I have hoped for."

I hung up the phone, went into the living room and told my husband, "You are not going to believe the telephone conversation I just had." God never ceases to surprise me. It was an answer to prayer. It was also an affirmation to hear that a young heterosexual couple was seeking a church that was open minded and welcoming of all people.

David and his girlfriend, Chanda, came to worship with us the following Sunday. I wanted him to experience the eclectic flavor of our congregation. The following week, he played the organ for worship. It was love at first note with David and the congregation!

One year into David's service with us he asked if we could have a private conversation. I sat down with a bit of trepidation. Maybe he had found a position that paid more. Maybe there was an organist position closer than the forty-minute drive from his home. David was a quiet, supportive colleague. I would hate to lose him as our organist. But I also wanted the very best for him. We sat down together after worship. Tentatively David wondered out loud "Do you think it would be possible for me to begin a choir?" My heart soared.

David and Chanda would go on to work tirelessly to create choral opportunities for the Bethel congregation. Many of the people in the choir could not read music. David 's skills as a teacher and choir director were amazing. He had ways to encourage every member of the choir. He even created opportunities for us to join with other small churches to sing cantatas. Never in my wildest dreams did I imagine that I would have the opportunity to work with a person of David's caliber. God had truly blessed Bethel once again.

12 - Extravagant Generosity

The extravagant generosity continues today. One thing I have learned in my ministry with Bethel is that extravagant generosity is not a one-time event. Extravagant generosity is a lifestyle; a way we approach the amazing gift of life. And yet each time it bubbles forth, I am surprised, humbled and just bit anxious.

One day I received a call from the Executive Director of Hoyleton Youth and Family Services, our partner organization who currently owns the building where we meet. They were in need of replacing a furnace in the building. The status of the unit had been tenuous for a long time. It actually caught fire last spring on a Sunday morning.

During worship the smoke alarm went off. In orderly fashion we exited the building. Once everyone was outside, the organist unplugged and picked up the organ and I picked up the communion elements. We talked, prayed and had communion in the parking lot as the volunteer firefighters took care of the faulty furnace.

The Director asked if there was a possibility we could donate some funds toward the purchase of the furnace. The good news was that it was September and we had yet to take money from savings to meet the budget that year. A gift toward the furnace would be a possibility.

The request was brought to the consistory. I had been thinking along the lines of a $500 gift. Five hundred dollars seemed to be a respectable amount for a church this size. In accordance with the churches bylaws, the consistory could authorize a gift of that amount. But that was not the direction the consistory wished to consider.

When the proposal was presented, there was immediate consensus we should help our mission partner. Someone asked how much money we had in savings. Someone else answered $10,000, with some in a CD and some in stock. Harry suggested we give Hoyleton a thousand dollars. I thought to myself "Is he crazy? That's 10% of all we have left. Is he thinking this is a tithe or is Harry just being extravagant? Maybe someone else will speak up and bring some practicality to the table."

Karen wondered aloud whether we shouldn't give them more. "They need it. We have it." Heads were shaking in affirmation. So Harry made a motion "I move we give Hoyleton $1,200 dollars." There was an immediate second. I reminded the consistory that expenditures of more than $500 required a vote of the congregation. "Well, then I guess this will just be a recommendation to the congregation."

Several weeks later a congregational meeting was held to vote on the proposed gift to Hoyleton for the furnace. Like most congregational meetings at Bethel, much of the discussion had already taken place around the refreshment table the prior week. Bethel uses a unique model for refreshment time. Each Sunday after worship, a different family of the church is responsible for bringing refreshments, something sweet and something healthy. Clara, the kitchen coordinator, makes sure there are paper items, coffee and Kool-Aid supplies. It is rare for a person not to linger after worship for refreshments at Bethel. This is a time to taste new recipes as well as openly discuss church and personal business. Instead of the private parking lot sort of conversation that sometimes happens at churches, Bethel members had already been openly discussing the options the church could offer Hoyleton.

Claudette, our consistory chairperson, opened the meeting and presented the topic of a gift to Hoyleton to help pay for the furnace. It was not a surprise when almost immediately we heard Harry's voice. "I move we give Hoyleton $1,500". Virgil seconded. I sat in disbelief; the gift had grown over the week. Claudette asked for discussion. A voice came from the back of the room " How much money is in our savings?" Finally a voice of reason or so I thought. "Roughly $10,000." Pat spoke up "Well, I think we should at least double that amount to Hoyleton. We have it. If it wasn't for Hoyleton we wouldn't be here." No one spoke. Claudette looked toward me. I think I had stopped breathing at that point. "Please God, help me," I silently prayed.

My next words shocked even me. "There is a motion on the floor that we need to vote on." Robert's Rules of Order to the rescue! Claudette continued "All those in favor of giving Hoyleton $1,500 say "Aye". Those opposed" – and there were none. Pat had a bit of a disappointed look on her face, which Claudette skillfully addressed by saying "We can always give Hoyleton more later on," to which Pat smiled.

Once again the congregation chose to give out of a sense of abundance, not a sense of scarcity, always thinking of the needs of others. A cautious person might ask, "How long can that go on? At some point all the money will be gone. Then they will have to close their doors." A Bethel member would tell you "Money is just one of many resources. We are called to be faithful with what we have today, and not worry about the future. The future will take care of itself."

A reminder of this happened the following week when the annual check arrived from a farmer who farms the remaining piece of land the church was given many years ago. We never know what the check will be; it all depends on the price of corn and beans in a given year. The amount is never considered a part of the church annual budget because it is always given away. Our rationale is that the farmland was given to us as a gift, so it wouldn't be right to keep the money from crops for ourselves. The annual check has usually been divided among several hunger projects throughout the area. Hunger projects seem to be the fitting recipients since the money came from farming.

When the check arrived, we were shocked. It was more than we had ever received - $1,700! The news washed over the consistory members like a holy affirmation that God is still speaking. It was a holy affirmation for living a generous lifestyle.

The immediate question was "Should we send the remaining $200 to Hoyleton?" After a few moments of conversation it was decided the Community Fund, which goes directly to people in rough times, was in desperate need of funds. With so many people out of work, we would undoubtedly need more money for that ministry. With one swift vote of the consistory, the community fund had a three-figure balance.

Postscript

The writing of this book marks the tenth anniversary of my ministry with Bethel Church. We continue to worship and actively participate in missions both local and global. Wonderful stories of stepping out in faith continue to unfold. We hope our story will lead others to step out in faith and then to share their stories with others. We believe God can and is using small membership churches to bring transformation to the world.

Let God use you and your congregation.

Prayer for Guidance

Loving God, You are our comfort and our prod, the one who will lead us beside still waters as well as encourage us to boldly step out onto stormy waters. We depend on You to walk with us and give us what we most need – comforting reassurance or a kick in the pants. Often we come to You with IF ONLY petitions. If only You would give us riches. If only You would give us more members to fill our pews. If only

_____ .

As we come to You in prayer, quiet our egos and fill us with the reassurance that You know what is best for us. Tenderly guide us as we set aside our "we've always done it that way" traditions. Move our focus away from our differences of opinion as we open our ears and our hearts to carefully listen to the passions and the concerns of one another.

Broaden our horizons, calm our fears and powerfully encourage us to step out in faith. We ask this in the name of our Savior, Jesus, who boldly walked on water, compassionately reached out to those outside his circle, and continually sought Your guidance through prayer. AMEN.

Conversation Starters

The first and foremost goal of this book is to tell the Bethel story.

In telling the story, it is my hope to be able to encourage and energize congregations on their journey of faith.

One of the key tools used throughout Bethel's story was congregational conversations. Open communication enabled all viewpoints, hopes and fears to surface. It was during person-to-person as well as congregational conversations that the deadly "If Only" thinking was uncovered. It was also during those conversations that "What If" thinking could be introduced and encouraged.

The following scriptures and questions are intended to serve as conversation starters for you and your congregation. If you email **shanks@htc.net** and let us know you are using this book with your congregation, the Bethel congregation and I will be praying for you and your congregation. Let the conversations begin!

Chapter 1: Persistence Pays Off

Luke 18:1-8

- Identify a time when persistence paid off for your church.

- What was the motivation behind that persistence?

Chapter 2: We Really Don't Have a Choice

Isaiah 41:13

- Identify a time when silence has drawn your church into despair.

- What was behind the avoidance? What are the "If only..." statements from your congregation?

Chapter 3: Choices

Joshua 23:1-8

- Identify times when you felt your church had no choices.

- What if you were challenged to discover possible choices for the future of your congregation? Who would you ask? Where would you look?

Chapter 4: Agency Dating

Psalm 32:8

- What if your congregation was looking for a ministry partner?

- Write a dating ad for your congregation as if they were seeking a partner.

- What would you be listening for in that first date with an agency?

Chapter 5: Hoyleton Imagines What's Possible

Ecclesiastes 4:9-12

- Identify your current partners in ministry.

- What if your congregation was challenged to strengthen those partnerships?

- Envision ten new possibilities to strengthen the partnerships.

Chapter 6: Details

Romans 13:8

- What would you find difficult about giving your church building away?

- What if your church made a will? Who would be named in the will and what would they receive? Writing a will might just help your congregation think outside the box.

.

Chapter 7: A Wedding at a Funeral

Psalm 100

- Who would you invite to your partnership celebration?

- What symbols of partnership might be included in the celebration?

Chapter 8: Selling the Farm

1 Timothy 6:17-19

- Identify a transformational moment of generosity within the life of your church? (A moment of not saving but transforming)

- What if your congregation chose to share $16,000 with ministry partners? What innovative ways would you create to share this gift?

Chapter 9: Youth Ministry With No Youth

James 1:22-25

- Identify an area of ministry not currently included in your church that you would like to add.

- List 10 ways to make that happen.

Chapter 10: A Power Pentecost

Isaiah 43:18-19 and Acts 2

- Can you identify an experience of being surprised by the movement of the Holy Spirit within the life of your church?

- In Isaiah 43 God says, "I am about to do a new thing." What new thing is God preparing to do in your congregation?

Chapter 11: A Musical Miracle

Psalm 100

- What role does music play in your church's worship service?

- Could the lack of musicians within a congregation lead to a premature death?

Chapter 12: Extravagant Generosity

Luke 6:37-38

- Can you identify a time your church felt affirmed for living a generous lifestyle?

- Name 7 partners whom your congregation is generous with.

- What if the two major "watch dogs" of the congregation's savings or endowment were gone? What new directions for generosity might be considered?

Author Biography

After thirty years of ordained ministry, Carol Shanks still loves the church. She has served as pastor in suburban, rural, and urban locations, with congregations ranging from 43 members to 1,826.

A graduate of Colorado State University and Iliff School of Theology, Carol finds great joy in helping people discover and use their passions to make a difference in the world. She finds these opportunities through her ministry as pastor, as well as Director of Admissions at Eden Theological Seminary and board member of Urban Mission Experiernce, www.umestl.org.

Your Notes